St Mary's University Press is an imprint of St Mary's University.
Its publications further the University's mission and values,
including excellence in research and scholarship.
St Mary's University Press is a registered trademark. Further details
can be found at www.stmarys.ac.uk/press/about.aspx.

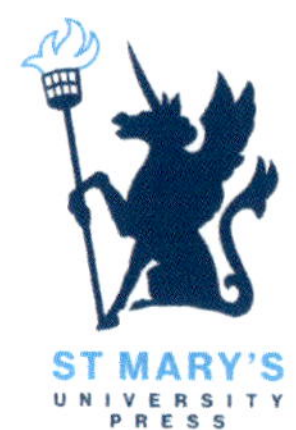

WINDOWS OF THE SOUL

Meditations on the Life of Mary in Stained Glass

Bishop Richard Moth

ST MARY'S UNIVERSITY PRESS

Published by St Mary's University Press
(www.stmarys.ac.uk/press/about.aspx)
in association with London Publishing Partnership
(www.londonpublishingpartnership.co.uk)

ISBN: 978-1-916786-09-7 (hbk)

A catalogue record for this book is available
from the British Library

Typeset in Adobe Garamond Pro by
T&T Productions Ltd, London
(www.tandtproductions.com)

Cover image

The cover shows 'The Coronation of Our Lady', one of the Loire windows at St Mary's University Chapel.

Credit: Sarah McKenna-Ayres.

To 175 years of Simmarians who – through their prayer, action and generous commitment – have made, and continue to make, St Mary's the leading centre of learning it is today

Contents

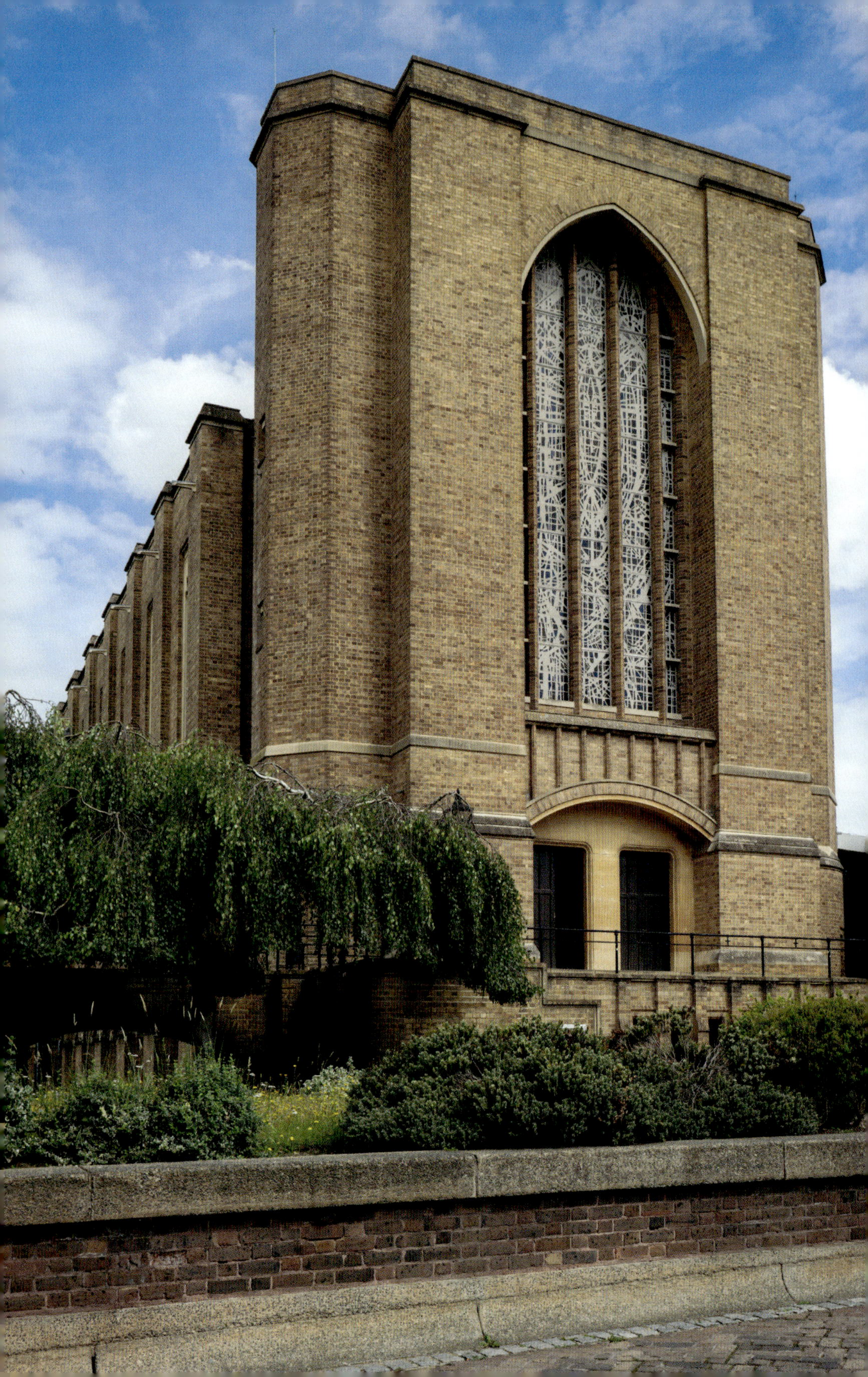

Foreword by Professor Anthony McClaran

As we celebrate the 175th anniversary of the foundation of St Mary's, it is good to reflect that there has always been a chapel at the heart of our institution: in our original home in Hammersmith; in the new college buildings that were constructed when St Mary's moved to Strawberry Hill a century ago; and, of course, at the heart of our university campus now, in the splendid chapel designed by Sir Albert Richardson at the beginning of the 1960s.

The chapel is the centre of so much that expresses St Mary's mission as a Catholic university: from the quiet daily Masses in crypt and main altar, and the festive celebrations of holy days and the Patronal Feast, to the joy and exuberance of our graduations, when we honour the achievements of our students and the work of our staff who teach and support them.

All those who have visited the chapel will know that the space is enhanced by the beautiful stained glass, made in the workshop of Chartres Cathedral and expressing through colour, shape and light the Mysteries of the Rosary. It is therefore very fitting that one of the ways in which we commemorate this significant anniversary for St Mary's is through this book. We are particularly grateful to our Chair of Governors, Bishop Richard Moth, for providing meditations and prayers to accompany the pictures of the windows themselves.

I hope that this book will be both a wonderful souvenir of the chapel and its magnificent glass and a source of inspiration, reflection and prayer for Simmarians past and present.

St Mary's University, August 2024

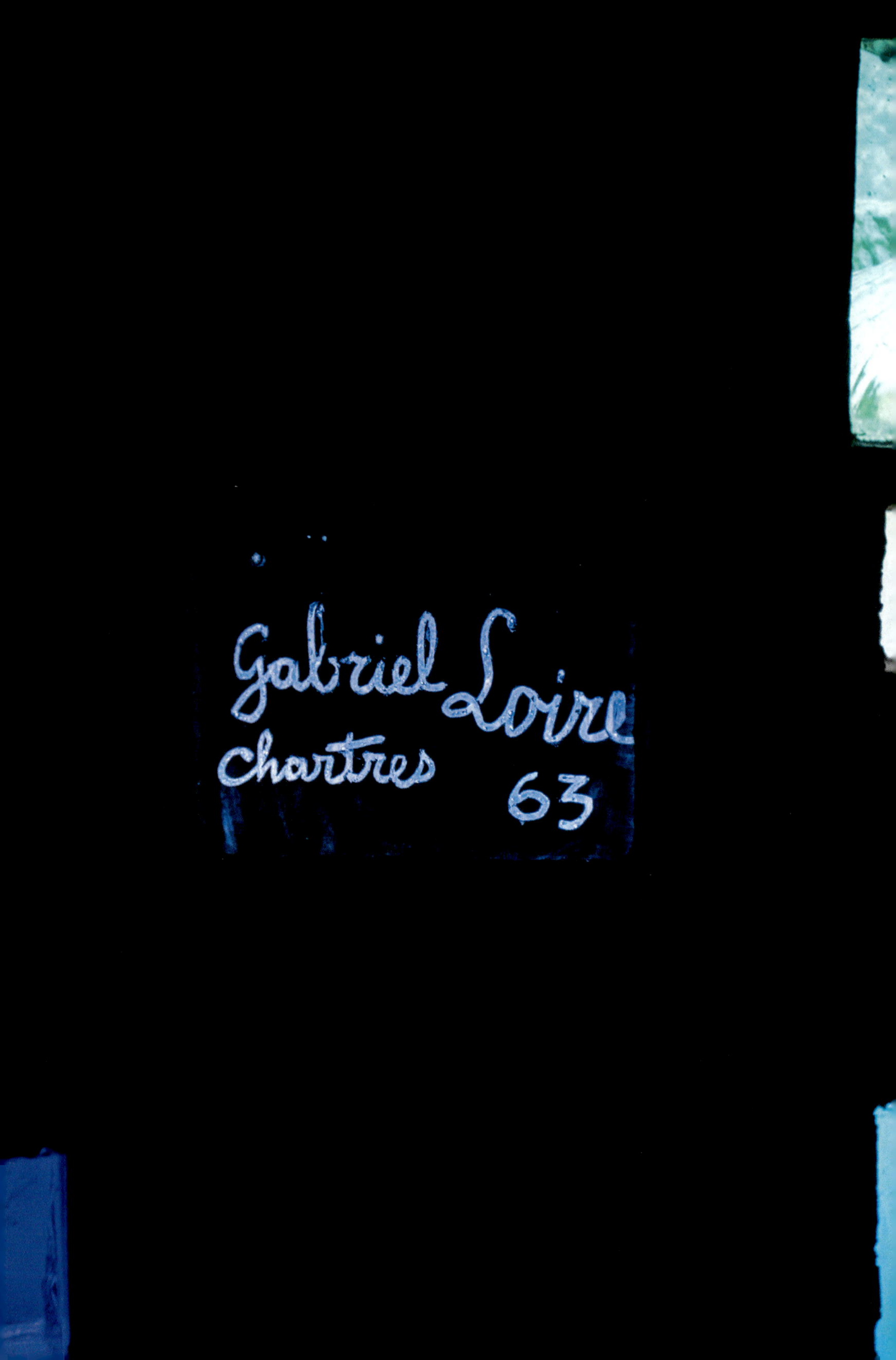

Gabriel Loire
Chartres
63

The Loire Windows at St Mary's University Chapel by Canon Dr Robin Gibbons

BACKGROUND

One of the first impressions one has on entering the St Mary's chapel is not only that of its vast rectangular space, but of the extraordinary quality of coloured light coming from the stained glass windows. It does not have a particularly British feel, and it immediately reminds one of the great French continental cathedrals with their medieval glass. If you visit Chartres Cathedral, you cannot help but notice the powerful effect that the interplay of light with the colours of the medieval glass has on the interior of the building, and therefore on tourist, worshipper and pilgrim alike. In particular, the red and blue glass has a depth that captures the imagination and tugs on the senses. A lot of this colour has been lost in the British Isles as one of the sadder factors of Reformation politics was the dismantling and destruction of a lot of medieval art, including stained glass. Fortunately, in the nineteenth and twentieth centuries good-quality glass craftwork reappeared in places such as the St Mary's chapel, but there is also a very direct connection between the university and Chartres: the windows were designed by Gabriel Loire.

GABRIEL LOIRE (21 APRIL 1904–25 DECEMBER 1996)

Loire was a French stained glass artist whose works appear in many venues around the world. He was the founder of the Loire Studio in Chartres, France, which continues to produce stained glass windows to this day. Loire was a leader in the modern use of 'slab glass' (*dalle de verre*), set in concrete. It is thicker and stronger than the stained glass technique of the Middle Ages, and this is what was used for the windows in the St Mary's chapel. The distinctive features of Loire's glass, made using this technique, are that the figures in his windows are mostly impressionistic in style and rich in colour.

Loire was born in Pouancé, France, on 21 April 1904. After completing his schooling in Angers in 1926, he went to a stained glass workshop in Chartres, which is where he learnt much of the ancient medieval technique of fusing colours in the glass itself, allowing him to capture the many variations of red, gold and blue colouring that are a distinctive feature of his works. Loire often expressed in his craft his own spiritual point of view that 'peace gives joy' ('*La paix donne la joie*'), particularly when working with shades of blue, which for him represented the colour of peace and the divine world. In 1946 he founded his own stained glass studio, the Atelier Loire, in Chartres, and this is still under the direction of his son, Jacques Loire, and his grandsons.

He died on Christmas Day in 1996, shortly after finishing a design for a new window. His works are displayed around the world. In addition to more than 450 installations in France, Loire's works are found in Great Britain, Germany, Ireland, South Africa, Japan, Chile, Canada, Australia and the United States, and we are privileged to have great examples of them at St Mary's.

A PERSONAL ENCOUNTER

When I was part of the theology and religious studies department at St Mary's, one of the courses I wrote and taught was called 'Religion and Art'. Part of the syllabus involved an examination of liturgical space and its components, so a regular lecture along with a following seminar were based in the St Mary's chapel, not least because it is an impressive example of church design in its own right and is historically important as one of the last religious buildings designed and built before the liturgical changes of the Second Vatican Council. The 1960s was a creative period in architectural development in Britain, and our chapel dedicated to Saint Mary and designed by Sir Albert Richardson was constructed in 1962–1963. Built in brick it is, in its scale and construction, much influenced by the early French Gothic brick-built cathedral of Albi in the Midi-Pyrénées region.

The highlight of our educational experience was always, however, the captivating presence of the diffused light from the stained glass windows and the intriguing abstract form of the themes of each, based on the Sorrowful, Joyful and Glorious Mysteries of the Rosary, including the hunt for the two signatures of Gabriel Loire himself.

The decision to continue the French influence, artistically, theologically and in the Marian symbolism, with the stained glass of the chapel windows, and to have them designed by Gabriel Loire and inserted into the chapel during its construction, was inspired. Part of my own teaching methodology was to utilize the building as an experience of what the designer of the glass intended: that is, to simply let the interplay of light and colour draw us into the imagery and to contemplate the symbols of the various Mysteries of the Rosary (Sorrowful, Joyful and Glorious). This took us beyond any lesson in design, art and colour, as the light of the many varieties of red and blue glass created an atmosphere of encounter and spirituality of transcendence. It was in this reflective and contemplative way that we examined and interpreted the Loire windows, dialoguing with them as Loire intended.

I remember an encounter with Sir Patrick Moore, the astronomer, during the recording of a programme that was to go out at Christmas. Both of us were leaning precariously over the choir balcony, so that the nativity window, with its star, could be the backdrop for shots of us. We were supposed to debate the veracity of the story of the Star of Bethlehem, but as both of us agreed on its meaning, our dialogue instead explored the abstract richness of the window, and as the winter light gradually faded, the nativity of Christ visibly touched those of us who were there, as the patterns of light changed, the reds receding into blackness and the white star shining ever clearly in the darkening gloom.

THE CONTEMPLATIVE SPIRITUALITY OF THE STAINED GLASS

There is a theme in Loire's contemplative schema. The chapel is dedicated to Our Lady, so the windows are based on the Mysteries of the Rosary, each one mirroring the methodical, contemplative rhythm of that prayer, each one a prayer in themselves. There are seven on each side of the nave, culminating in the glorious Mystery of the Crowning of Our Lady in the great west window.

The intensity of colour is profound: blue of heaven, red of earth and human life including martyrdom, gold of holiness, and white mediating the divine presence. I found that a good equivalent spiritual expression of our windows can be found in the words of others. Rudyard Kipling, for example, provides us with a detailed account of the experience of how this art form works on mind and soul – one that allows us to see how our glass can be experienced in a similar manner.

The Kiplings were driving through France on 13 March 1925, having visited Rouen to see the 11,000 graves at the war cemetery. Later that same day they visited the Church of Our Lady at Les Andelys and the cathedral at Evreux. In a letter written to the novelist H. Rider Haggard the following day, Kipling wrote of the stained glass at Les Andelys:

> Colour, old man, is what, *au fond*, clinches a creed. Colour and the light of God behind it. That's as near as Man will ever get.*

In the late afternoon of the 13th, the family arrived at Chartres, and after his visit Kipling wrote the following:

> Got into the Cathedral – on the very last fading of the twilight – and it was as though one moved within the heart of a Jewel of the Faith. You know the inexpressible colour glories of Chartres – all the windows superb and some without flaw or blemish in any aspect. Last time I'd seen it the glass was all out… Now all the glories were returned – rose window and all – and in that last few minutes of darkness overcoming day, the windows burned and glowed like the souls of martyrs. Don't know when I've been more touched in the deeps.

The intensity of the experience moved him to write a sonnet on Chartres, the opening lines of which I hope will also speak to those of us who can also see that touch of Chartres in the windows of Gabriel Loire in the St Mary's chapel:

> Colour fulfils where Music has no power:
> By each man's light the unjudging glass betrays
> All men's surrender, each man's holiest hour
> And all the lit confusion of our days.

In a very real sense, what Kipling is describing here is at the heart of the philosophical and theological ethos behind the work of Gabriel Loire.†

* Pinney, Thomas (ed.). 2004. *Letters of Rudyard Kipling*, volume 5, p. 212. Macmillan.

† The background and source material for Kipling's sonnet on Chartres can be found on the website of the Kipling Society at www.kiplingsociety.co.uk/readers-guide/rg_chartres1.htm.

THE WINDOWS' SPIRITUAL LEGACY

When looking at our Loire windows and their religious themes, we need to remind ourselves that the stained glass in our church buildings essentially has a threefold purpose (in addition to the obvious material one of allowing daylight to penetrate the interior while preventing adverse weather conditions from entering).

First, it has a deeply theological rationale: the quality of the light itself allows us to enter the metaphor of St John's Gospel, for the glass emphasizes the light itself as the symbol of divine presence permeating the world (John 8:12): 'I am the light of the world. Whoever follows me will never walk in darkness, but will have the light of life.' This is, as John also proclaims in his prologue, the true light of Christ present among us in our encounter of worship and prayer, bathed in the light of our windows (John 1:4,5): 'In him was life, and the life was the light of humanity. And the light shines in the darkness, and the darkness did not overcome it.'

A second purpose of stained glass is both didactic and illustrative: that of making visible the story of our salvation, in order to both inspire and impress the faithful. This is because images tend to make things more 'real' than is the case with mere discourse – the colours and patterns focus our attention and leave a subtle message or a general impression on the person who sees them.

A third purpose of the stained glass window is to visually embrace the interior, drawing the space together, so that the building may be perceived as a unity and, therefore, a microcosm of celestial Jerusalem, far from the distractions of the world. This is part of the great spirituality inherent in our engagement with stained glass, for it elevates our senses in a physical manner, making us look up and beyond, allowing us to see the divine light mediated through colour and glass. Additionally, through the experience of the light and its atmosphere, it creates a new expression of relationship with the divine world, which, like music, opens in us the condition for contemplative prayer.*

*

The windows are impressive works of art and enormously important examples of the oeuvre of Gabriel Loire, whose contribution to the design and craft of

* I have to thank the online blog 'The spirit of the eye' for helping me articulate these three aspects. See https://visual-worlds.org/2021/03/17/contemporary-stained-glass-windows-the-glory-of-nevers/.

stained glass windows is second to none and deserves far wider recognition than it has previously received.

However, Loire's windows at Saint Mary's are more than simply glorious pockets of explosive colour: they are a spirituality of the visual, of our own encounter with the divine world through colour and light – a method of prayer that was well known in the medieval period and resurrected by Loire in his works. Though our windows at St Mary's are abstract in form, they are also distinctively part of the great liturgical and artistic symbol structure of the Catholic world and a glorious treasure in themselves. In this respect, Bishop Richard's meditations, enshrined in this book, are a worthy expression of that moment where light and colour, faith and transcendence, theology and hope all meet.

Chamole, France

WINDOWS OF THE SOUL

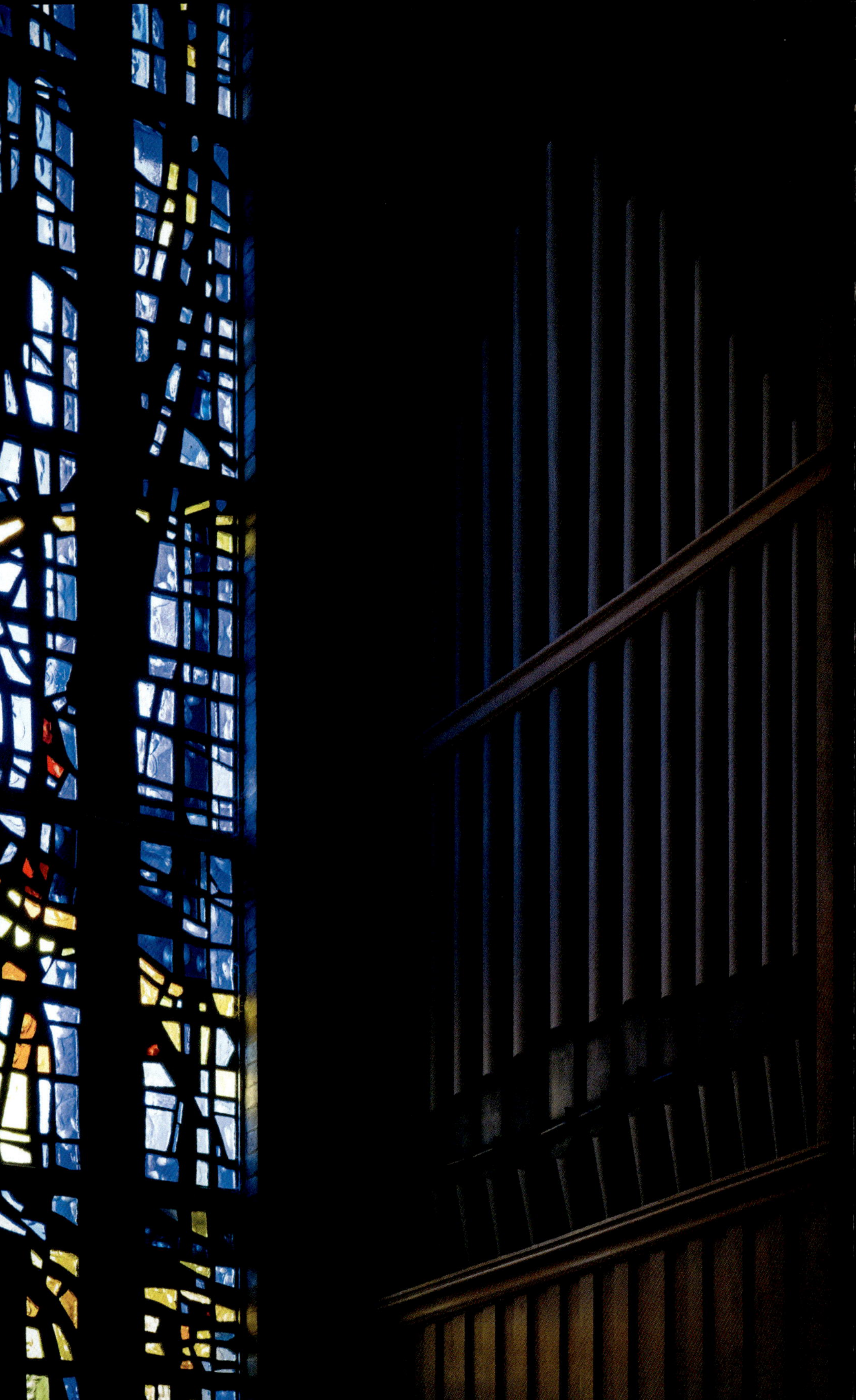

Introduction

The chapel at St Mary's University stands at the centre of its Strawberry Hill campus and is a wonderful reminder of the core principles of the University, which was founded by the church and continues its teaching and research work as a Catholic university.

The chapel is a gift both for the University and for the wider community. Not only do its windows – fine works of art by the French stained-glass artist Gabriel Loire – enhance the building, they are also a call to prayer and reflection on the Mysteries of the Rosary. It therefore seems appropriate to mark the 175th anniversary of the University – and the centenary of its arrival at Strawberry Hill – with a publication focusing on Loire windows that might assist with prayer and reflection.

I do hope that the scripture texts and the short meditations on each mystery that follow this introduction will assist prayer and, perhaps, prove helpful both to those who pray the rosary regularly and to those who are new to it.

May the intercession of Mary our Mother, and the patron of our University, continue to bring many graces to all who are associated with St Mary's.

THE JOYFUL MYSTERIES

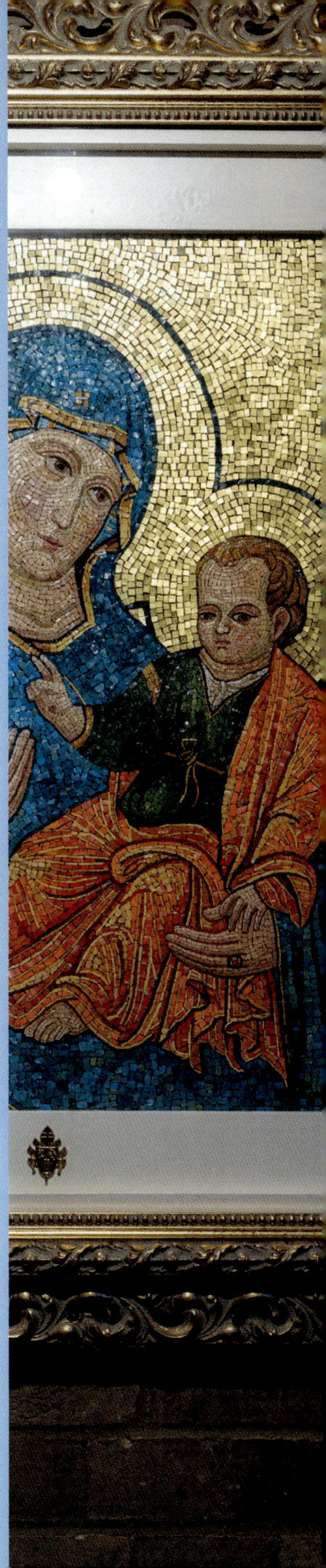

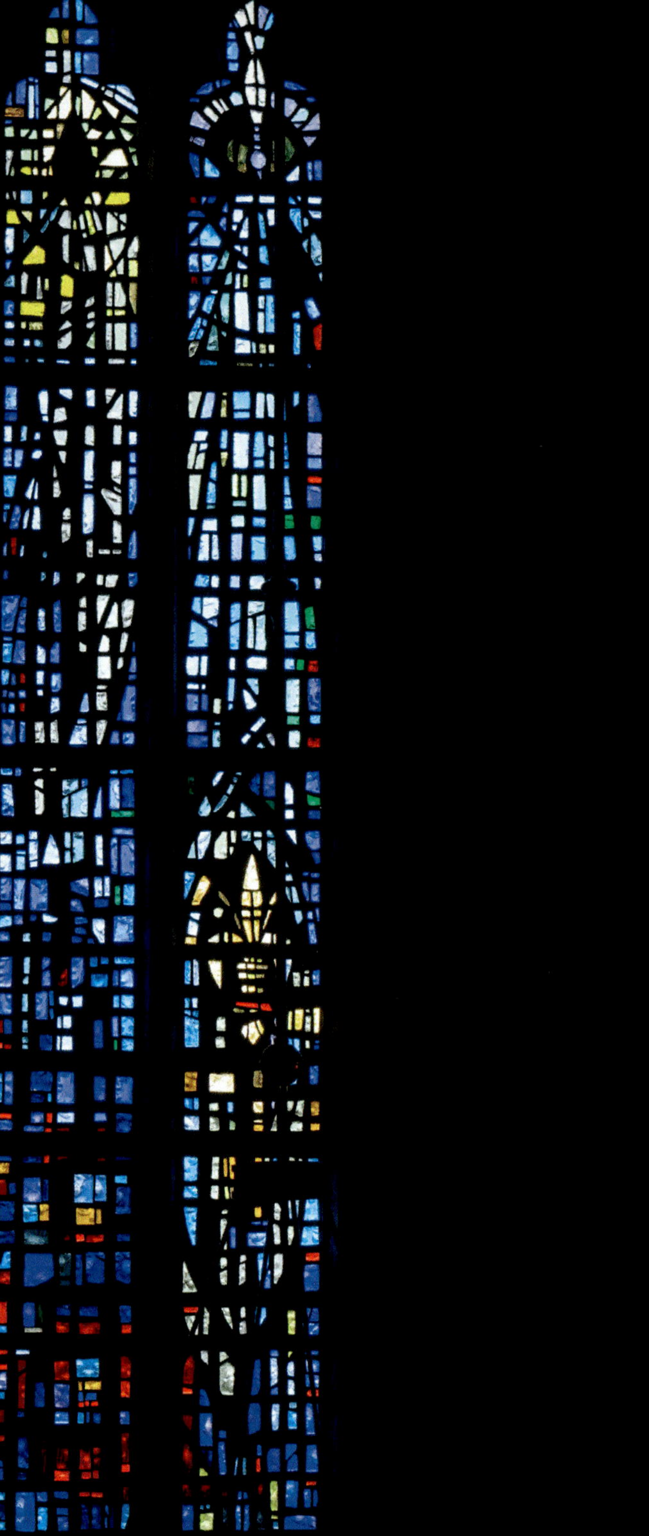

The Annunciation

In the sixth month, the angel Gabriel was sent from God to a city of Galilee named Nazareth, to a virgin betrothed to a man whose name was Joseph, of the house of David. And the virgin's name was Mary. And he came to her and said, 'Greetings, O highly favoured one, the Lord is with you?' But she was greatly troubled at this saying, and tried to discern what sort of greeting this might be. And the angel said to her, 'Do not be afraid, Mary, for you have found favour with God. And behold, you will conceive in your womb and bear a son, and you shall call his name Jesus. He will be great and will be called the Son of the Most High. And the Lord God will give to him the throne of his father David, and he will reign over the house of Jacob for ever, and of his kingdom there will be no end.'

And Mary said to the angel, 'How will this be, since I am a virgin?'

And the angel answered her, 'The Holy Spirit will come upon you, and the power of the Most High will overshadow you: therefore the child to be born will be called holy – the Son of God. And behold, your relative Elizabeth in her old age has also conceived a son, and this is the sixth month with her who was called barren. For nothing will be impossible with God.' And Mary said, 'Behold, I am the servant of the Lord: let it be to me according to your word.' And the angel departed from her.

Luke 1:26–38

*

Our words in the 'Hail Mary' are those of Gabriel: 'Hail, Mary, full of grace the Lord is with thee.'

Gabriel brings the message – but it is the Holy Spirit Who is active. The image of the dove coming upon Mary – represented by the fleur-de-lis – is seen in simple, light colours, suggesting the mystery of this event.

The Annunciation marks the beginning of our salvation, for the Word is made flesh in Mary from this very moment. Mary is *Theotokos*, the bearer of God. She carries the Saviour, Who is God-with-us.

The mystery of God's action in our lives is often difficult to grasp. Like Mary, we must discern what it is that is God's call for us. The call is to a response of simplicity and trust, and Mary teaches us this too: 'Let it be to me according to your word.'

As with Mary, so the Spirit is active in us. In our own small ways, we too are 'bearers of God' – called to bring God's light and love to the world and to recognize that same light burning in all whom we meet.

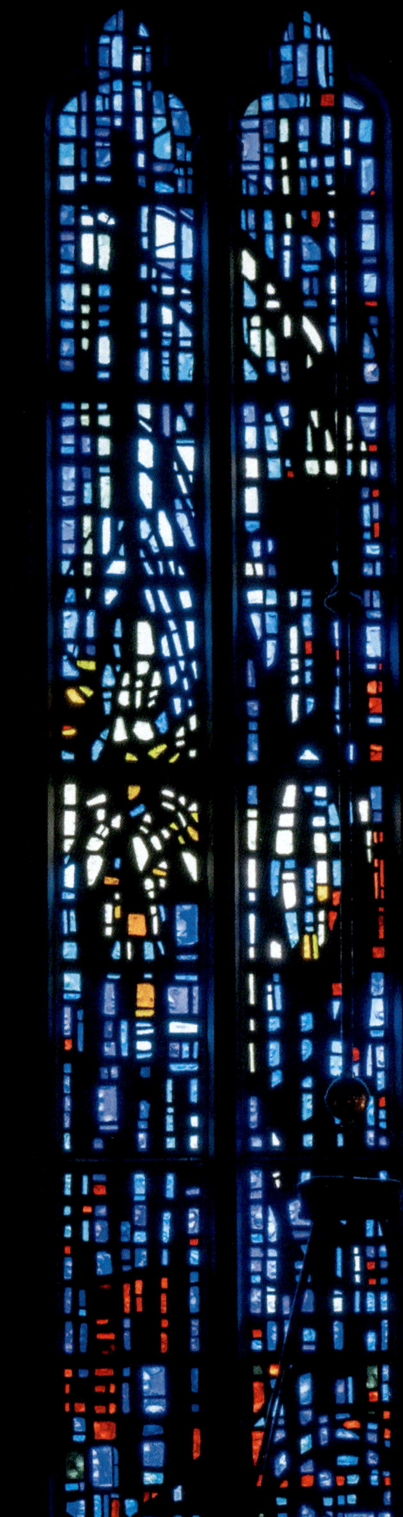

The Visitation

In those days Mary arose and went with haste to the hill country, to a town in Judah, and she entered the house of Zechariah and greeted Elizabeth. And when Elizabeth heard the greeting of Mary, the baby leaped in her womb. And Elizabeth was filled with the Holy Spirit, and she exclaimed with a loud cry, 'Blessed are you among women, and blessed is the fruit of your womb! And why is this granted to me that the mother of my Lord should come to me? For behold, when the sound of your greeting came to my ears, the baby in my womb leaped for joy. And blessed is she who believed that there would be a fulfilment of what was spoken her from the Lord.'

Luke 1:39–45

*

Elizabeth continues, as it were, the prayer begun by the angel: 'Blessed art thou among women and blessed is the fruit of thy womb, Jesus.' The glass of this window represents Elizabeth bowing towards the Saviour, in the womb of Mary.

There is, in this meeting, the wonder of recognition beyond that of Mary and Elizabeth for each other. The leap of Elizabeth's child – the movement in her womb of John, who is to be known as 'the Baptist' – is the leap of joy at the presence of the Saviour.

Elizabeth rejoices, not only that Mary has made the difficult journey to visit her but that Mary has believed and accepted the wonder of God's plan for her.

Even when the plan that God has for us is a challenging one, may we rejoice in it, knowing that this is the way for us to become the people we are called to be. Let us rejoice, too, in the plans God has for others – recognizing their dignity and the particular place God has for them in His divine plan.

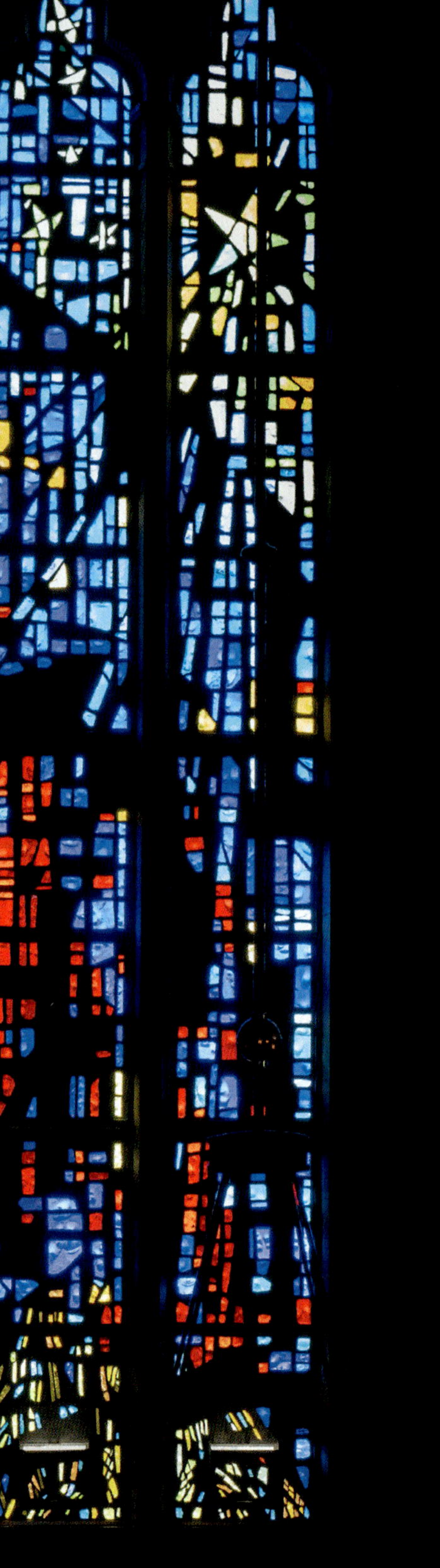

The Nativity

In those days a decree went out from Caesar Augustus that all the world should be registered. This was the first registration when Quirinius was governor of Syria. And all went to be registered, each to his own town. And Joseph also went up from Galilee, from the town of Nazareth, to Judea, to the city of David, which is called Bethlehem, because he was of the house and lineage of David, to be registered with Mary, his betrothed, who was with child. And while they were there, the time came for her to give birth. And she gave birth to her firstborn son and wrapped him in swaddling cloths and laid him in a manger, because there was no room for them in the inn.

Luke 2:1–4

*

The star of Bethlehem shines bright in this window – bringing light to the darkness of the place of Jesus' birth and pointing the way for all who come to visit Him Who is the Light of the world.

Yet, the Saviour is born in poverty, in the shelter for the animals, where Mary and Joseph retreat to the innermost recesses of the cave of Bethlehem for warmth and privacy. It is not the rich and famous who are the first to hear of His birth, but the shepherds. It will not be long before He is a refugee, to be 'called out of Egypt' only when Herod is dead.

Can it really be true that God comes amongst us in this way? Most certainly, for God's ways are not our ways, His thoughts not our thoughts. The Saviour of the world, King of kings and Prince of peace is born in simplicity, poverty and rejection. If only the people of Bethlehem realized Who was born amongst them!

The jubilation of the shepherds as they hear the singing of angels must surely be our jubilation also. The very poverty of Jesus' birth is a source of joy, for it speaks of the very purpose of His coming (Luke 4:18–19): 'To proclaim good news to the poor, to proclaim liberty to captives and recovering of sight to the blind, to set at liberty those who are oppressed, to proclaim the year of the Lord's favour.'

As we rejoice and proclaim the birth of the Saviour, may we be bearers of the light of His mercy and new life to all.

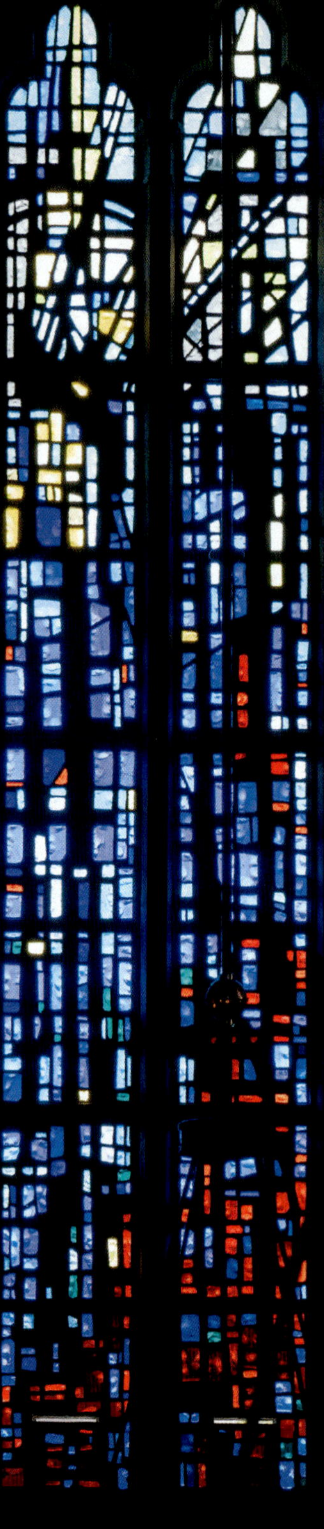

The Presentation in the Temple

And when the time came for their purification according to the Law of Moses, they brought him up to Jerusalem to present him to the Lord. Now there was a man in Jerusalem whose name was Simeon, and this man was righteous and devout, waiting for consolation of Israel, and the Holy Spirit was upon him. And it had been revealed to him by the Holy Spirit that he would not see death before he had seen the Lord's Christ. And he came in the Spirit unto the temple, and when the parents brought in the child Jesus to do for him according to the custom of the Law, he took him up in his arms and blessed God and said,

> 'Lord, now you are letting your servant depart in peace,
> according to your word;
> for my eyes have seen your salvation
> that you have prepared in the presence of all peoples,
> a light for revelation to the Gentiles,
> and for glory to your people Israel.'

Luke 2:22, 24–32

*

Light shines on the steps of the temple in Jerusalem, as we gaze at this window. Simeon sees the Light of the world made flesh in the Christ child – himself enlightened by the Holy Spirit, Who prompts him to go to the temple. It is little wonder that the Feast of the Presentation is also Candlemas – the day when candles are blessed for churches and homes.

The Christ is the light for Whom Simeon has waited, not just for a little while but for the whole of his life. Christ calls us to Himself and in Him we find fulfilment and the meaning for our lives for which we all seek.

The Light of the world is for all peoples – just as Simeon expresses it – and in our own age, we are the bearers of that light. The closer we come to Christ, the more we fulfil the work He has for us, the more we shall be able to say with Simeon 'My eyes have seen your salvation' – for we are called to be the servants of the One Who is born for us.

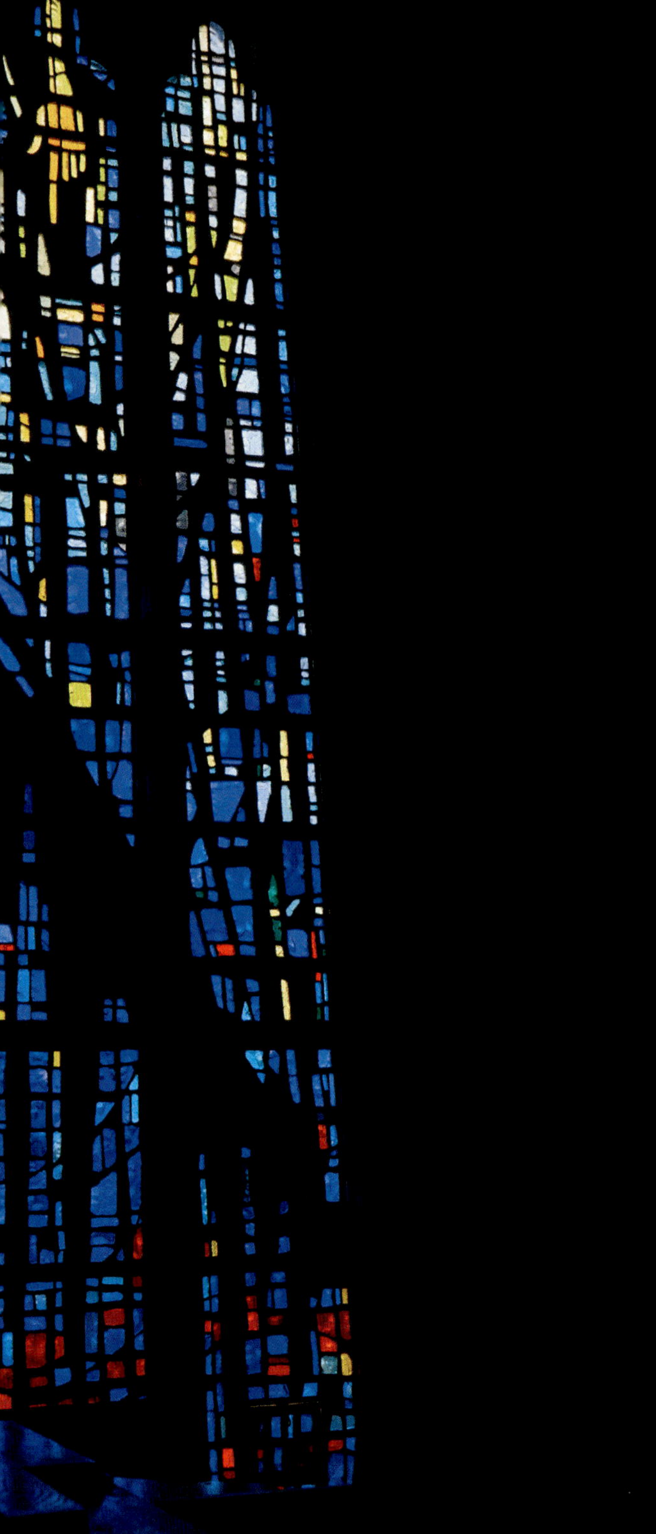

The Child Jesus among the Doctors

Now his parents went to Jerusalem every year at the Feast of the Passover. And when he was twelve years old, they went up according to custom. And when the feast was ended, as they were returning, the boy Jesus stayed behind in Jerusalem. His parents did not know it, but supposing him to be in the group they went a day's journey, but then they began to search for him among their relatives and acquaintances, and when they did not find him, they returned to Jerusalem, searching for him. After three days they found him in the temple, sitting among the teachers, listening to them and asking them questions. And all who heard him were amazed at his understanding and his answers.

Luke 2:41–47

*

The image of Jesus' hand is prominent in this window, shedding light as He teaches us.

Just as the doctors of the Law, with whom the young Jesus spoke and debated, were amazed at His wisdom and answers, are we not also amazed at the wonder of His message to us? All through the Gospel, the Lord invites his hearers to a deeper understanding of the ways of the Father. This is often disturbing and not all can accept His teaching.

Those called to the vocation of teaching are called to mirror the action of Jesus: enabling those who listen to them to move to places of deeper understanding and knowledge. All this is done that we may know the wonder of God more deeply.

This was the insight of Mary of Bethany, who realized that the opportunity to sit at the Lord's feet and listen was a chance not to be missed. May we be open, always, to the depths of understanding that comes from sitting with Jesus and listening to Him.

THE SORROWFUL MYSTERIES

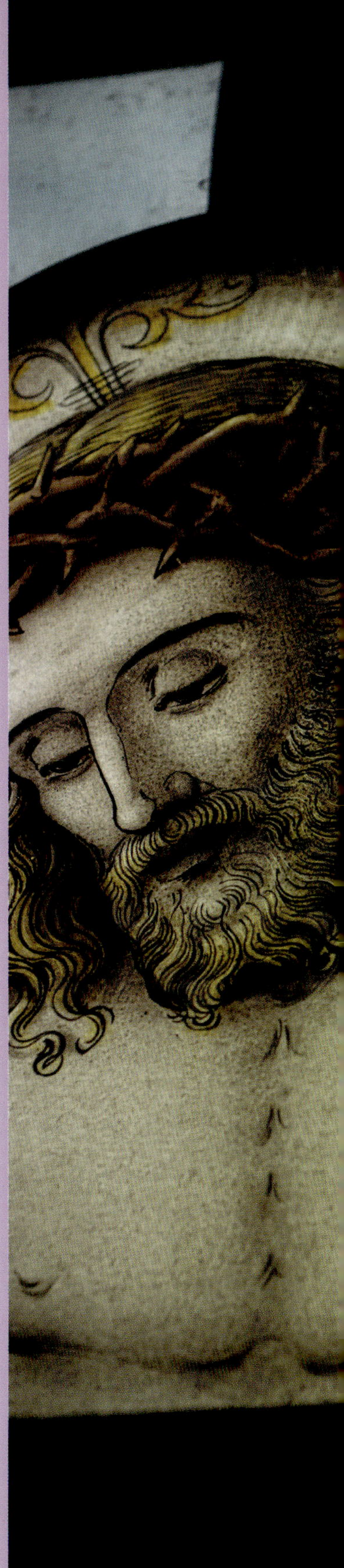

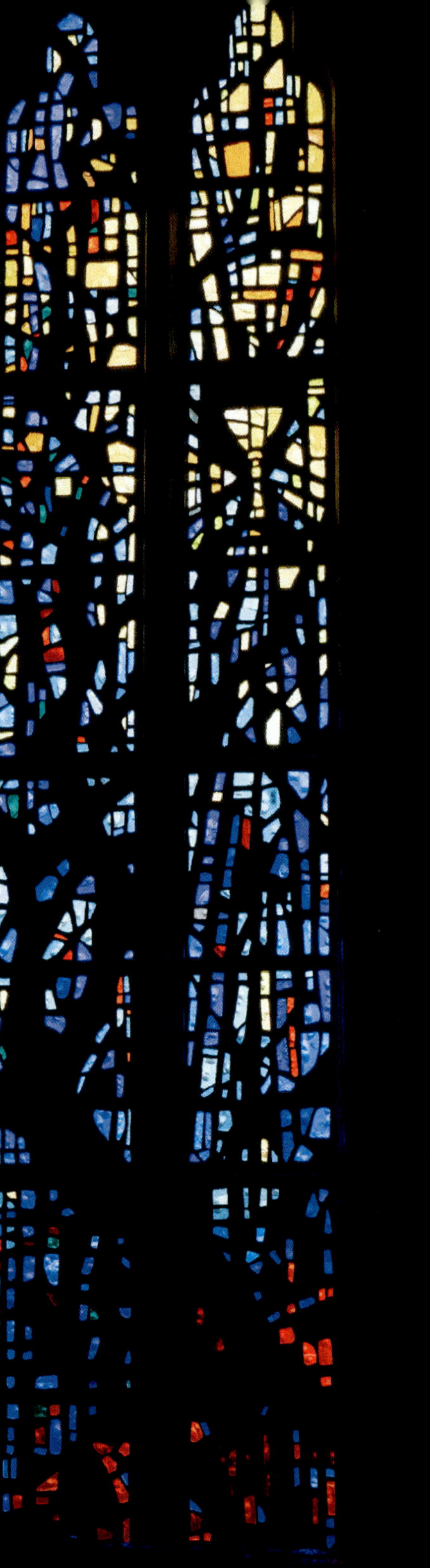

The Agony in the Garden

And he came out and went, as was his custom, to the Mount of Olives, and the disciples followed him. And when he came to the place, he said to them, 'Pray that you may not enter into temptation.' And he withdrew from them about a stone's throw, and knelt down and prayed, saying, 'Father if you are willing, remove this cup from me. Nevertheless, not my will, but yours, be done.' And there appeared to him an angel from heaven, strengthening him. And being in agony he prayed more earnestly; and his sweat became like great drops of blood falling down to the ground.

Luke 22:30–44

*

As the time for the fulfilment of His mission of salvation approaches, the people ask (John 11:56): 'What do you think? That he will not come to the feast at all?' Jesus does, of course, come to Jerusalem and, having celebrated the Last Supper with his disciples, faces the reality of all that is to come in his prayer of anguish before the Father.

The image of the cup of suffering, from which he is soon to drink, shines into the darkness of the glass of this window. It is all the Lord can see, as He prays and his anguish is beyond our imagining.

When faced with the prospect of suffering, or even the greater or lesser trials of life, we may find ourselves in anguish. The grace of God is a source of strength at such times – just as the angel brought strength to the Lord. With His grace, even the most daunting thing, the most acute suffering, can become a source of blessing for us and for others.

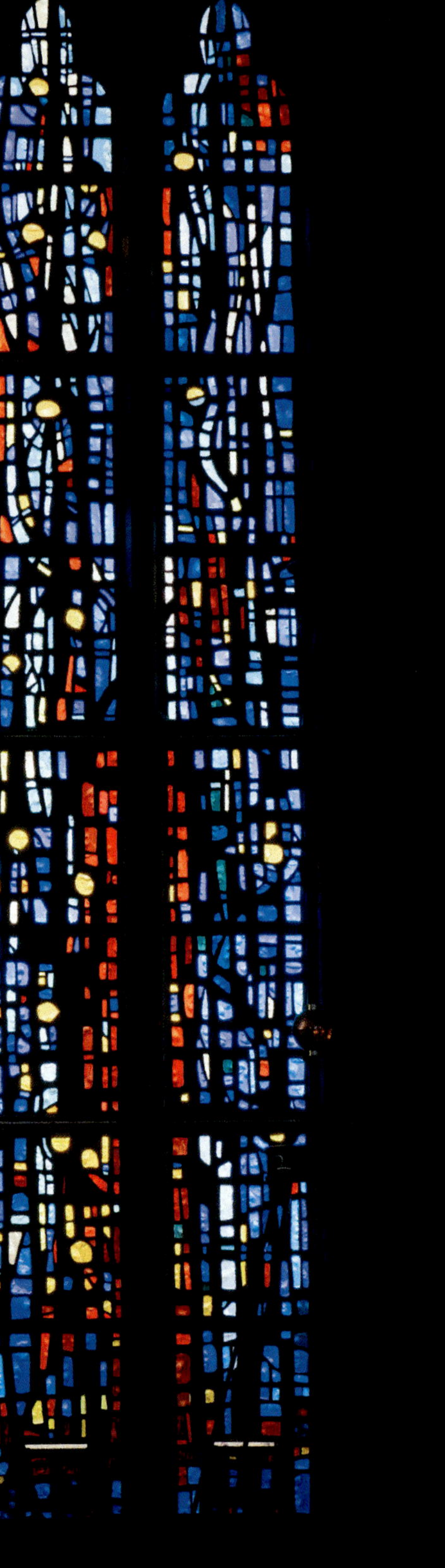

The Scourging at the Pillar

So when Pilate saw that he was gaining nothing, but rather that a riot was beginning, he took water and washed his hands before the crowd, saying, 'I am innocent of this man's blood; see to it yourselves.' And all the people answered, 'His blood be on us and on our children!' Then he released for them Barabbas, and having scourged Jesus, delivered him to be crucified.

Matthew 27:24–26

*

The images of the blood-soaked pillar and the weighted scourges, seen in this window, invite us to ponder on this seemingly needless brutality.

Pilate had wanted Jesus scourged and then released, but his weakness led him to give the order for Jesus' crucifixion. The scourging was also a preliminary to the torture of the cross, since this, together with the carrying of the cross, weakened the one condemned to death.

There was no avoiding this brutality. How often are we guilty of inflicting needless brutality on others? How often do we wield the scourge of violence, let alone the scourge of language – sometimes meted out by others on our behalf? The pointless violence of the scourging is reflected in so many ways across our society and our world, and Jesus dies for every one of these offences, in every place and at every time in history.

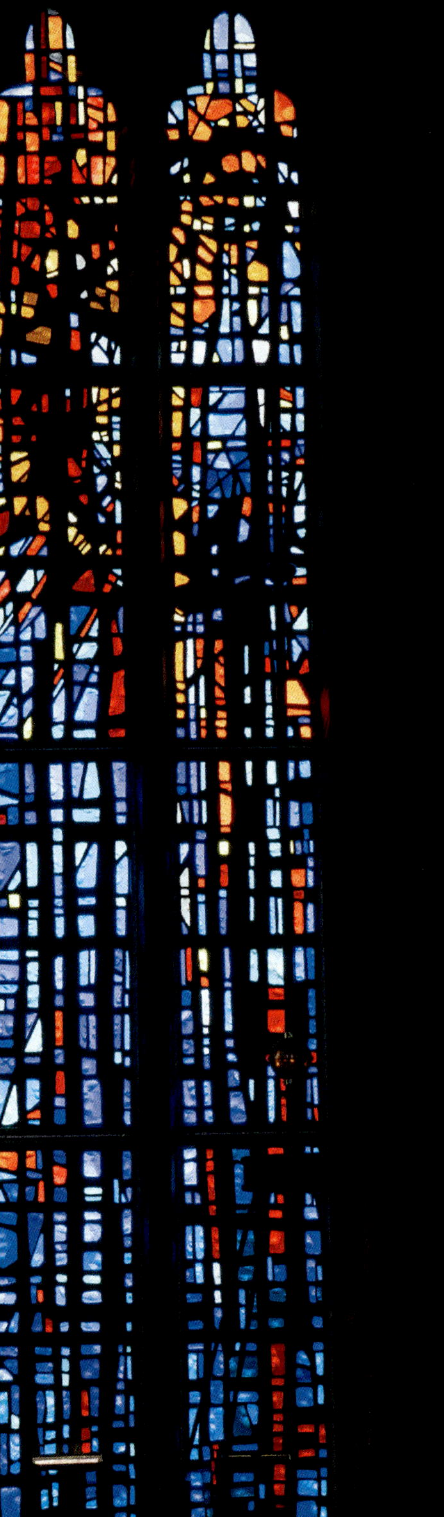

The Crowning with Thorns

And the soldiers twisted together a crown of thorns and put it on his head and arrayed him in a purple robe. They came up to him, saying 'Hail, King of the Jews!' and struck him with their hands. Pilate went out again and said to them, 'See, I am bringing him out to you that you may know that I find no guilt in him.' So Jesus came out, wearing the crown of thorns and the purple robe. Pilate said to them, 'Behold the man!'

John 19:1–5

*

The crown of thorns would have been made with the spiny branches of the acacia tree – its spines often more than an inch in length – causing the Lord further pain and loss of blood. The dark circlet of the crown of thorns takes its place in this window.

The soldiers who dressed Jesus in the purple colour of kings and mocked Him so cruelly did so simply for their own entertainment. This was not part of the punishment and death ordered by Pilate – it was purely gratuitous. What is more, the soldiers' amusement at Jesus' expense is brought out for the crowd to see.

Jesus' response is one of silent acceptance. He has no one to defend Him, for his friends have deserted Him. He is voiceless with the voiceless, vulnerable with the vulnerable, abused with the abused.

He Who is the Light of the world, the One who is without sin, takes on our lot, our experience, our sufferings – in the way of silent love.

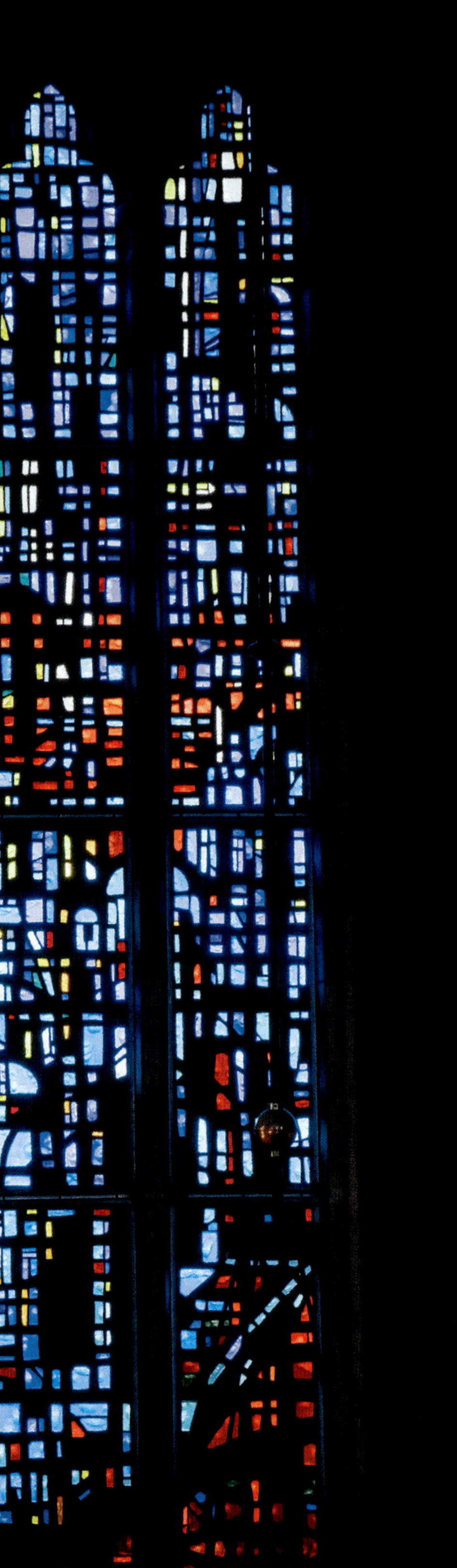

The Carrying of the Cross

And when they had mocked him, they stripped him of the purple cloak and put his own clothes on him. And they led him out to crucify him. And they compelled a passerby, Simon of Cyrene, who was coming in from the country, the father of Alexander and Rufus, to carry his cross.

Mark 15:20–21

*

Jesus carries the cross – most likely, the beam of the instrument of His death – up the hill towards Golgotha. The image of this hill of struggle and pain, seen at the bottom of the window, is set against the background of the domed houses of the city of Jerusalem.

Simon of Cyrene, who makes only this one appearance in the Gospel narrative, is an instrument of mercy in an otherwise brutal and piteous situation. Mark alone amongst the Gospel writers records the names of Simon's sons. The writer of the shortest Gospel, it seems, wanted to be sure that Simon is remembered, along with the example he was to his family and to all who would come after him.

Mercy is a necessary quality of the follower of Christ. Simon is an example for us to follow – are we not called to be the Simons of our own age? Are we not called to lift the burdens of others, to help them carry the weight of their crosses?

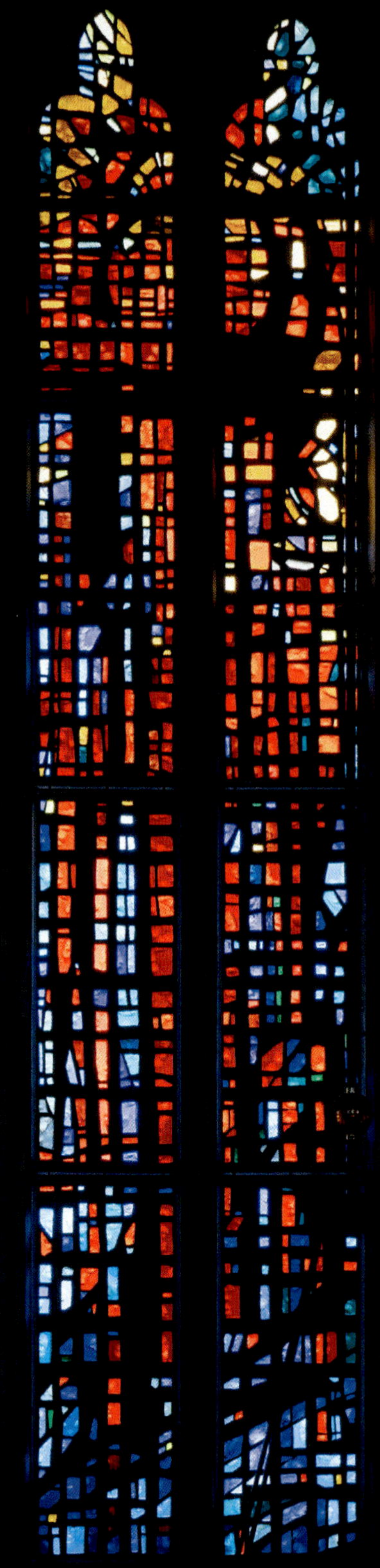

The Crucifixion

And when they had crucified him, they divided his garments among them by casting lots. Then they sat down and kept watch over him there. And over his head they put the charge against him, which read, 'This is Jesus, the King of the Jews.'

Matthew 27:35–37

*

The image of the cross is created not by the glass of this window but by its stone mullion. The cross stands out, dark, solid, foreboding. Behind it, we see the corona of light that is the sign of Christ's victory over suffering and death.

The world spins on its axis, and we add to its motion, as it were, through our frenetic human activity: our looking here and there for the answers to our questions, forever seeking new things, often missing the point altogether or seeking solace where no comfort is to be found.

In the midst of this activity, the Cross of Christ stands – ever present and calling us to reflect upon its significance and upon the One Who hung and died upon it out of love for us.

Stat crux dum volvitur orbis – the Cross stands while the world goes round. This insight from the Order of Carthusians is helpful for us. The Cross calls us to stop and reflect. This is not easy, but we must come to learn how to be at home at the foot of the Cross. There we are with Mary, John and Mary Magdalene. There we gaze on the mystery of Salvation, on the victory over sin and death. Remaining here, with the Mother of Jesus, brings grace and peace.

THE GLORIOUS MYSTERIES

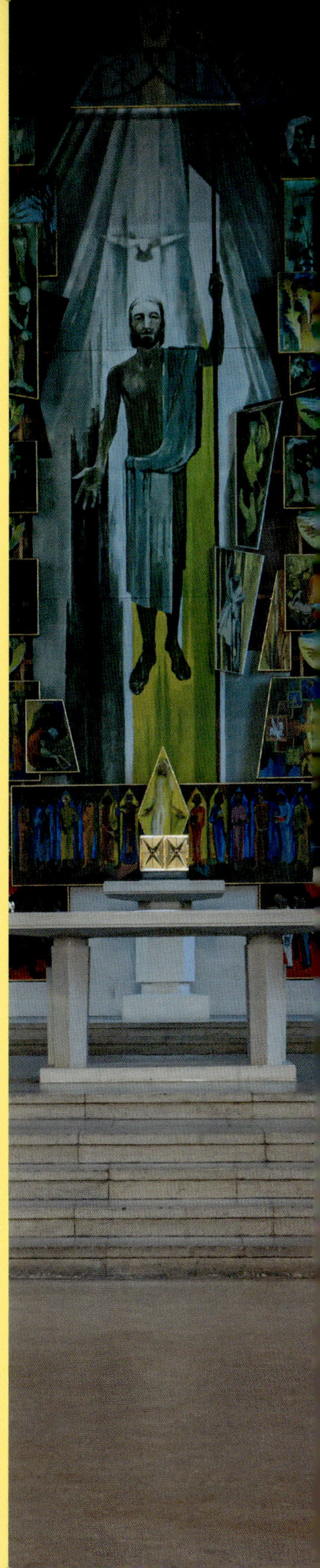

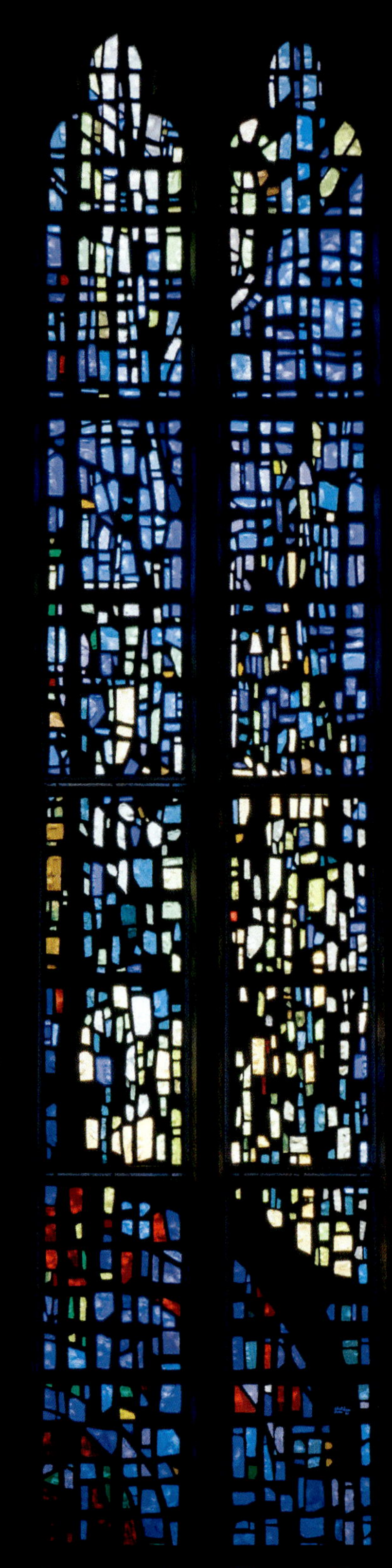

The Resurrection

Now on the first day of the week Mary Magdalene came to the tomb early, while it was still dark, and saw that the stone had been taken away from the tomb. So she ran and went to Simon Peter and the other disciple, the one whom Jesus loved, and said to them, 'They have taken the Lord out of the tomb, and we do not know where they have laid him.' So Peter went with the other disciple, and they were going to the tomb. Both of them were running together, but the other disciple outran Peter and reached the tomb first. And stooping to look in, he saw the linen cloths lying there, but did not go in. Then Simon Peter came, following him, and went into the tomb. He saw the linen cloths lying there, and the face cloth, which had been on Jesus' head, not lying with the linen cloths but folded up in a place by itself. Then the other disciple, who had reached the tomb first, also went in, and he saw and he believed.

John 20:1–8

*

The darkness of the tomb, represented at the bottom of the window, gives way to the light of the Resurrection Morn. Christ is Risen. Alleluia!

As we reflect on the moment for which the whole of creation waits, we stand with Mary Magdalene. We cannot easily grasp and understand the reality of Jesus' resurrection from the dead. Perhaps, for us, it can take a lifetime to appreciate just what Jesus does for us in his life, death and resurrection.

Peter, the impetuous one, does not share the hesitation of the young John. He is not afraid to enter the tomb. He sees; he takes it all in. However, it is John, the beloved disciple, who truly grasps the reality of things – and believes.

In a world that is ever-increasingly complicated and where simplicity is often suspect, may we learn from John.

Eight days after the resurrection, Jesus will say to Thomas (John 20:27): 'Do not disbelieve, but believe.' Thomas's response must surely give hope and confidence to us, in our present age (John 20:28): 'My Lord and my God!'

The message of the resurrection is Good News, for it is life for the world. Let us not be afraid of John's simplicity, Mary Magdalene's wondering, Peter's grasp of things and Thomas's profession of faith – and may we be confident in confessing the resurrection before the world.

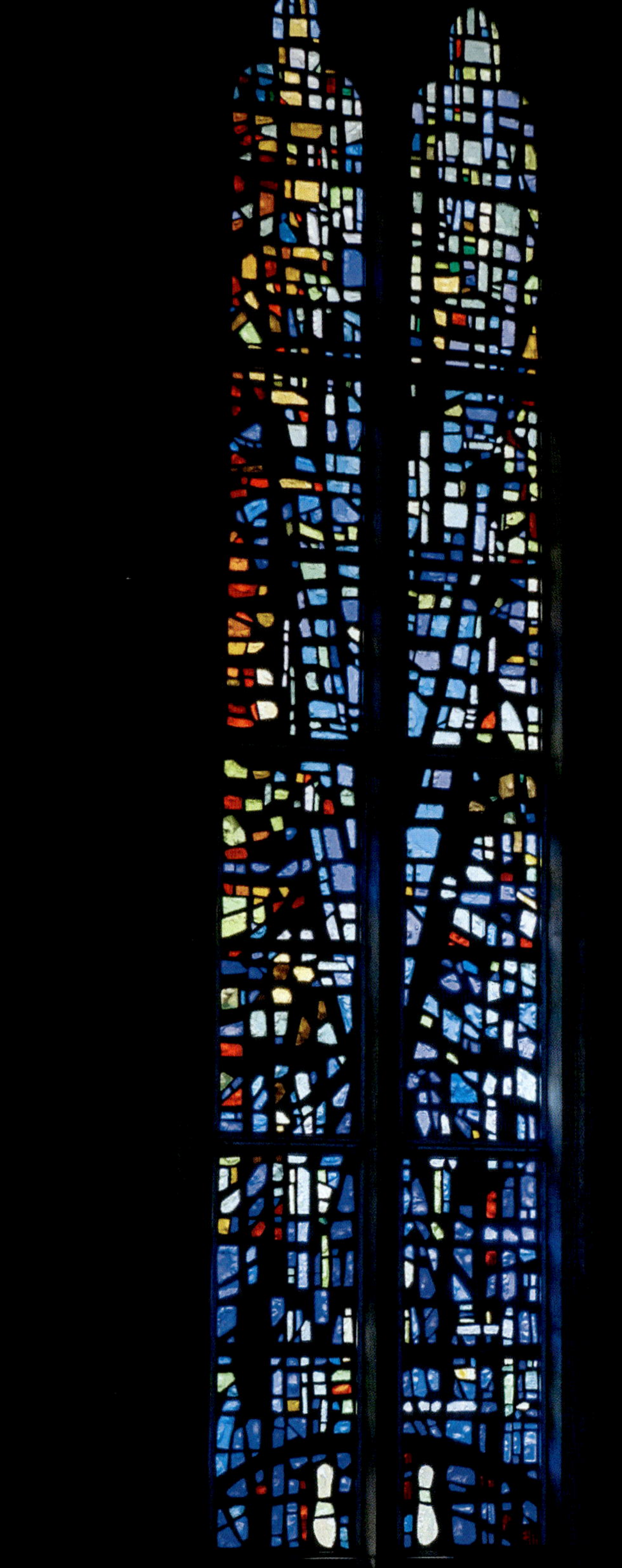

The Ascension

And he had them out as far as Bethany, and lifting up his hands he blessed them. While he blessed them, he parted from them and was carried up into heaven. And they worshipped him and returned to Jerusalem with great joy, and were continually in the temple blessing God.

Luke 24:50–53

*

The light of this window has a purity and simplicity, with the marks of Christ's feet at the very bottom of the glass, indicating his return to the Father.

Jesus had told the disciples that he must return to the Father, for only then will He send the Holy Spirit. Why are the disciples not saddened by his parting? They are filled with the joy of his resurrection and their response to Jesus' ascension is one of worship, joy and praise.

In the Acts of the Apostles, the same Luke who wrote the Gospel records that the angel told them that they would see Him return – a further cause of joy and peace for the disciples.

It is difficult for us to place ourselves in this moment of ascension, for the Holy Spirit has come upon the Church and we are now living in that age before the Lord's return. As we pray during the celebration of the Eucharist (Roman Missal, Communion Rite, n. 124): 'We await the blessed hope and the coming of our Saviour, Jesus Christ.'

Hope is a mark of the Christian, for our eyes look always to the coming of Christ and, while we await in hope, we are called to build His Kingdom here on earth. May we be trusting in our hope and filled with the joy and praise that we see in the disciples.

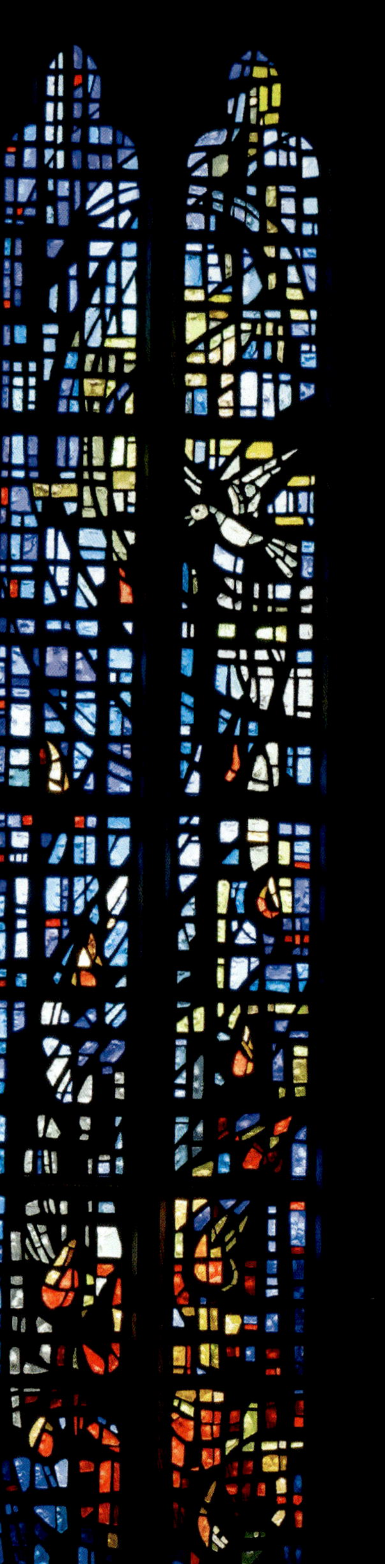

The Descent of the Holy Spirit

When the day of Pentecost arrived, they were all together in one place. And suddenly there came from heaven a sound like a mighty rushing wind, and it filled the entire house where they were sitting. And divided tongues of fire appeared to them and rested on each of them. And they were all filled with the Holy Spirit and began to speak in other tongues as the Spirit gave them utterance.

Acts 2:1–4

*

The Holy Spirit who comes upon Mary at the moment of the Annunciation, who is seen in the form of a dove at the Baptism of Jesus, comes now to the disciples. The image of the dove in the window is accompanied by the swirling pattern of wind and the tongues of fire that rest upon Jesus' followers.

The action of the Holy Spirit is decisive. The response on the part of the disciples is immediate, for their fear has gone and they are gifted with all that is necessary for the proclamation of the Good News. No matter what may come their way, they will persevere, facing persecution and martyrdom in their response to the gift of the Holy Spirit. They will have an eloquence that they had never known before and the impact of their mission will not fail.

Just as Mary, at the moment of the Annunciation, gave her 'yes' to God, so – under the guidance of the same Holy Spirit that came to her – the disciples will go wherever they are called to be.

This sense of urgency must be present in us, as we seek to be ever more open to the Lord's call to us. The Lord has given us the task of proclaiming His life to the world. If all is done under the guidance of the Holy Spirit, the work will always be fruitful.

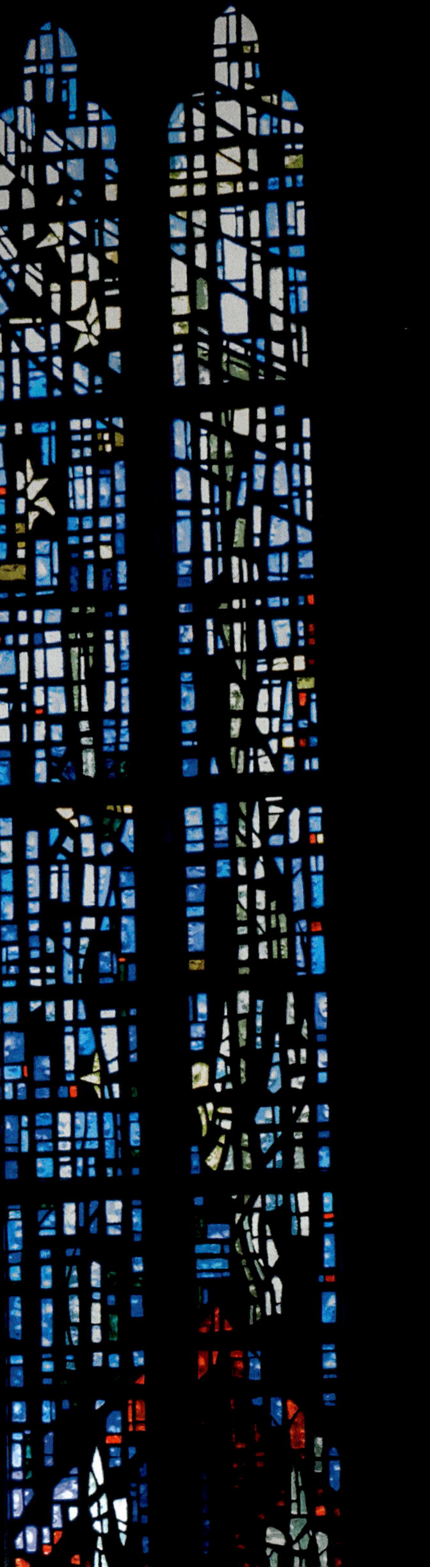

The Assumption

'My soul magnifies the Lord, and my spirit rejoices in God my Saviour,
for he has looked on the humble estate of his servant.
For behold, from now on all generations will call me blessed:
for who is mighty has done great things for me, and holy is his name.
And his mercy is for those who fear him from generation to generation.
He has shown strength with his arm;
he has scattered the proud in the thoughts of their hearts;
he has brought down the mighty from their thrones
and exalted those of humble estate;
he has filled the hungry with good things,
and the rich he has sent away empty.
He has helped his servant Israel, in remembrance of his mercy,
as he spoke to our fathers, to Abraham and his offspring for ever.'

Luke 1:46–55

*

The image of the fleur-de-lis is seen again in this window, rising to become stars of light in the glass.

Mary's special place in the plan of Salvation meant that she would not undergo the corruption of the grave, but would share in the grace of her Son's resurrection at the point of her death, experiencing the 'blessed hope' of her Son's coming at the moment of her 'falling asleep'.

Truly, the wonder of her hymn of praise at her meeting with Elizabeth is fulfilled. The Almighty has indeed done great things for Mary and holy is his name.

Mary's Assumption is, as the preface of the Assumption describes, 'a sign of sure hope and comfort to your pilgrim people'. She is 'the beginning and image of your Church's coming to perfection' (Roman Missal, preface of the Assumption).

As God has done great things in Mary, so He will do great things in and for us – calling us to the wonder of His Kingdom of justice, light and peace.

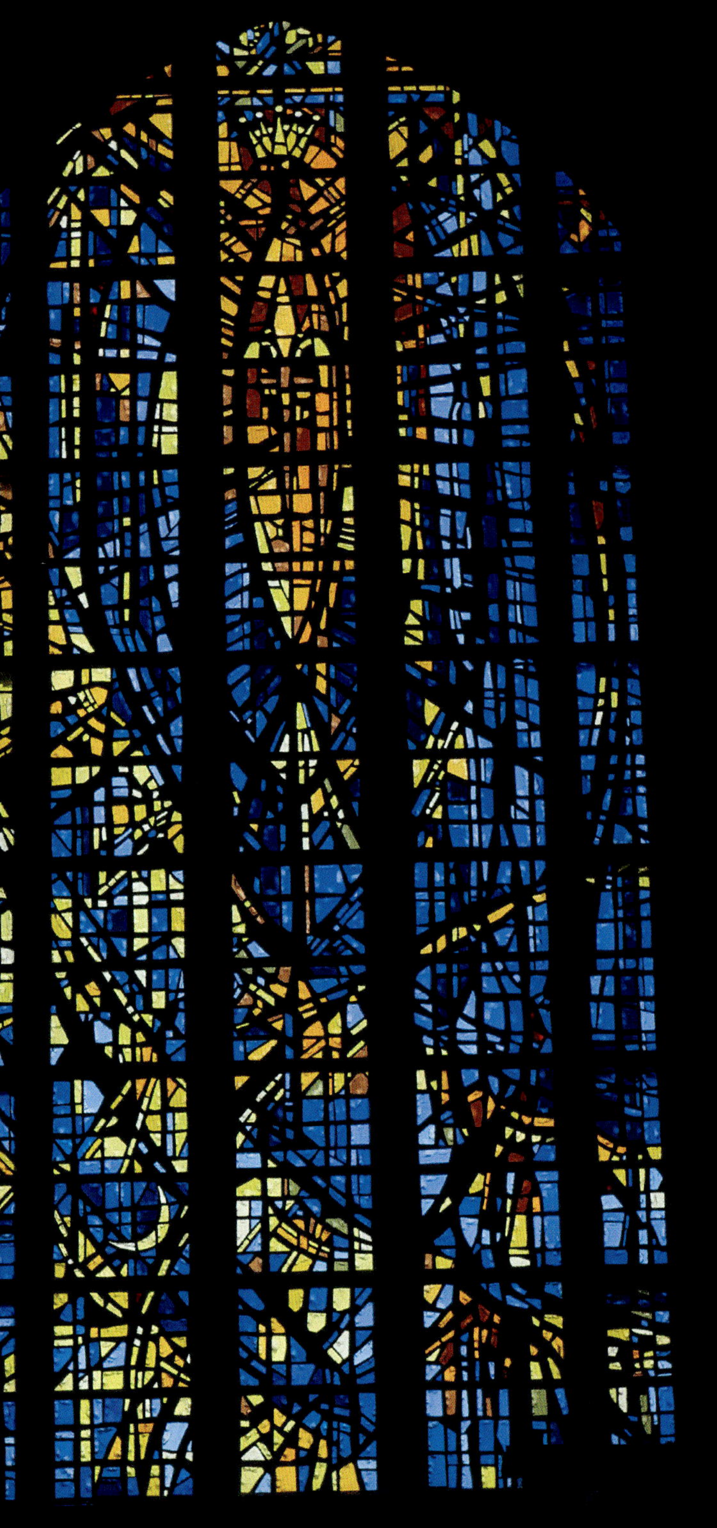

The Coronation of Our Lady

And a great sign appeared in heaven: a woman clothed with the sun, and with the moon under her feet, and on her head a crown of twelve stars.

Revelation 12:1

*

The great west window of the chapel provides a wonderful image in glass of the place that Mary our Mother has in the Kingdom of Heaven. She is living in the eternal light of the Blessed Trinity – seen above the fleur-de-lis that symbolizes her and the Crown that is the mark of her queenship. She is surrounded by angels.

This is the fitting place for the *Theotokos*, the bearer of God, the one who gave birth to the Word made flesh, the Saviour of the world – she who followed his every step to the foot of the Cross, who rejoices in His resurrection and was with the disciples as the Holy Spirit came.

Where Mary – a human being like us – has gone, we are called to follow. Through our own positive response to His call and through lives of prayer and service, may we too know the wonder of Heaven.

The 15 Mysteries in the Life of Our Lady by Gabriel Loire

JOYFUL MYSTERIES

1. The Annunciation
2. The Visitation
3. The Nativity
4. The Presentation in The Temple
5. The Child Jesus among the Doctors

SORROWFUL MYSTERIES

6. The Agony in the Garden
7. The Scourging at the Pillar
8. The Crowning with Thorns
9. The Carrying of the Cross
10. The Crucifixion

GLORIOUS MYSTERIES

11. The Resurreection (and the signature of G. Loire)
12. The Ascension
13. The Descent of the Holy Spirit
14. The Assumption
15. The Coronation of Our Lady

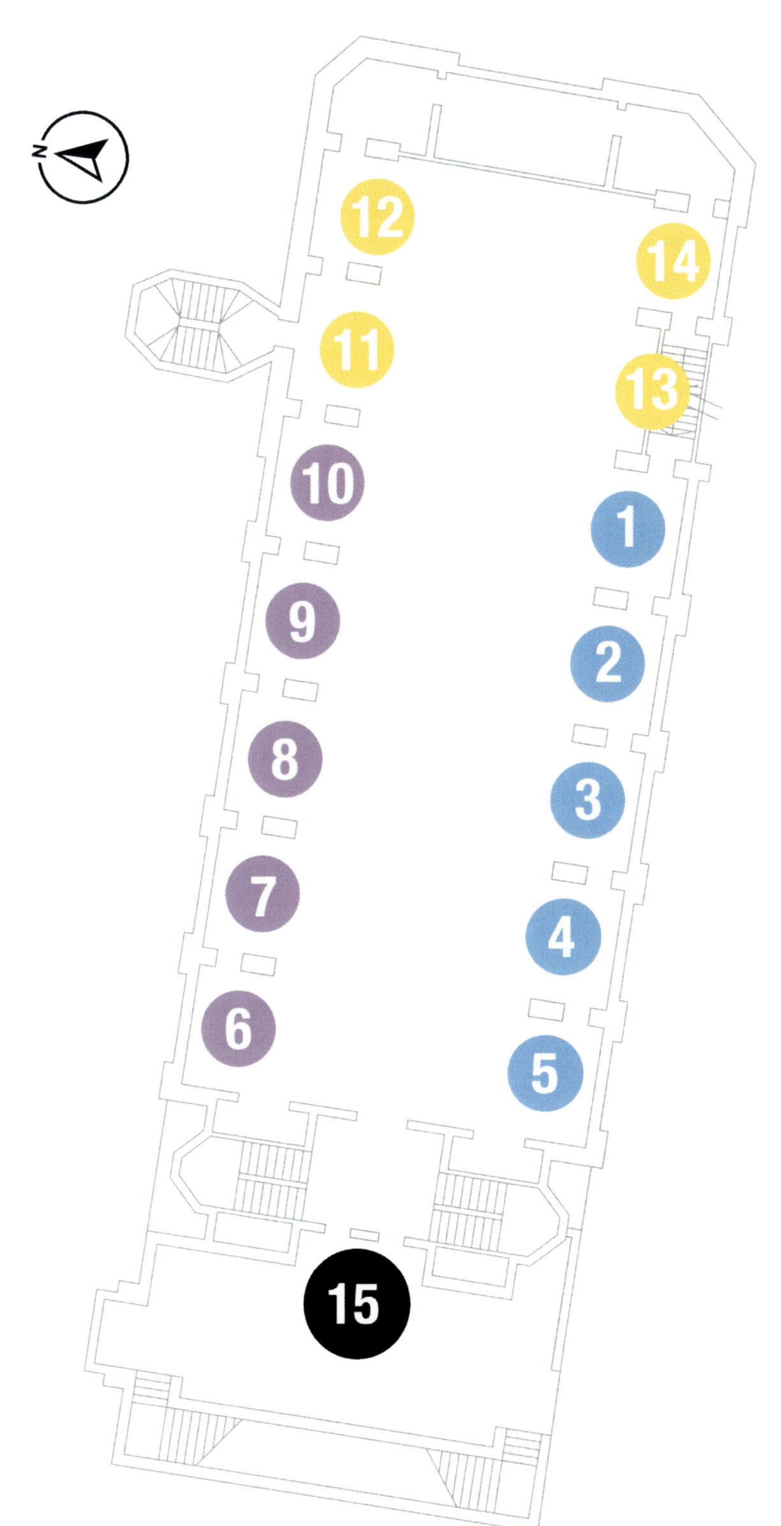
N
12
14
11
13
10
1
9
2
8
3
7
4
6
5
15

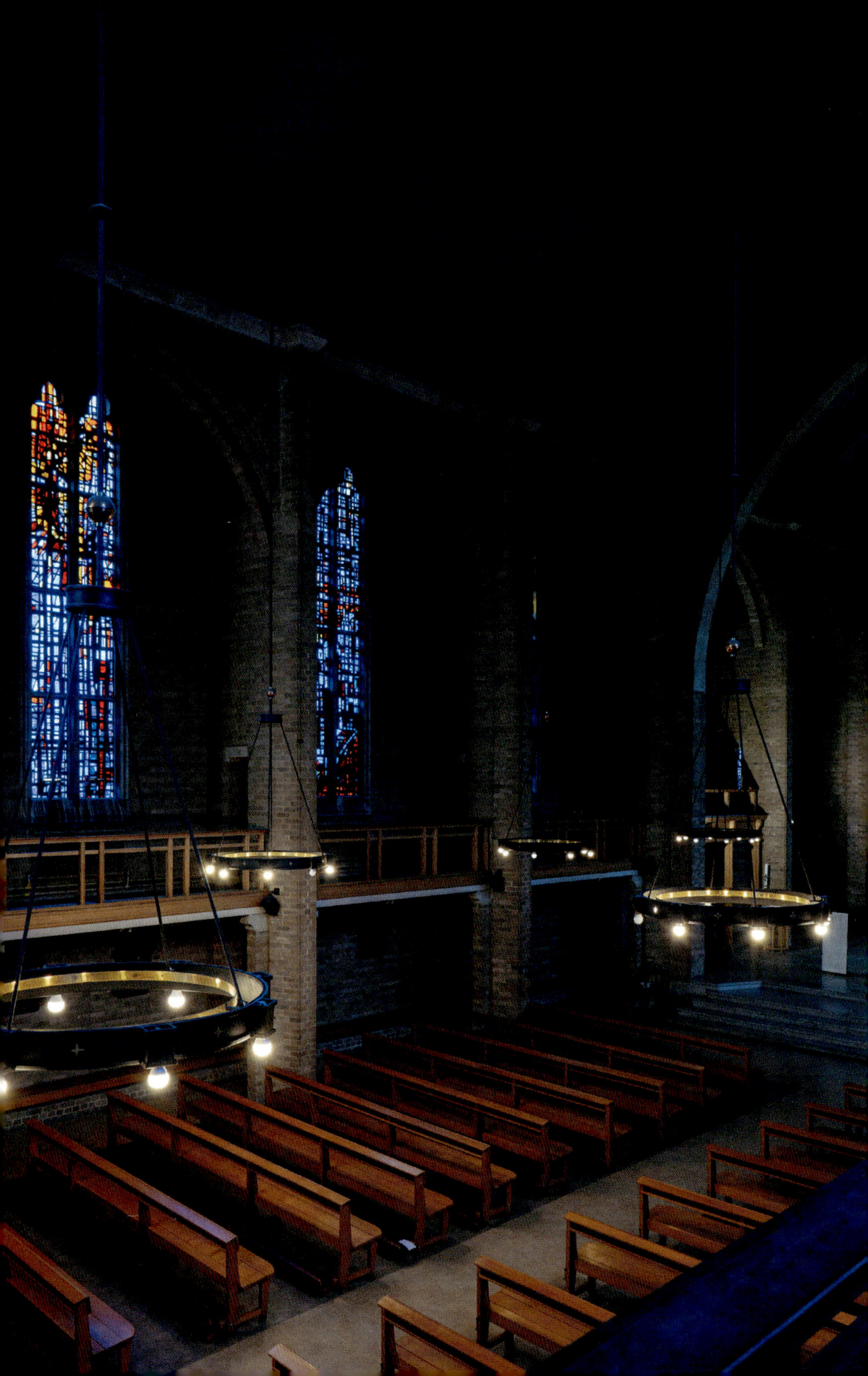

Acknowledgements

I am grateful for the kind assistance and support of St Mary's University Press in bringing this book to fruition. In particular, I would like to thank Richard Baggeley, Sam Clark, Peter Tyler, Kim Salmons and Michelle Paull. I am also grateful for the support of St Mary's Chaplaincy and the team there, headed by Canon Peter Newby.

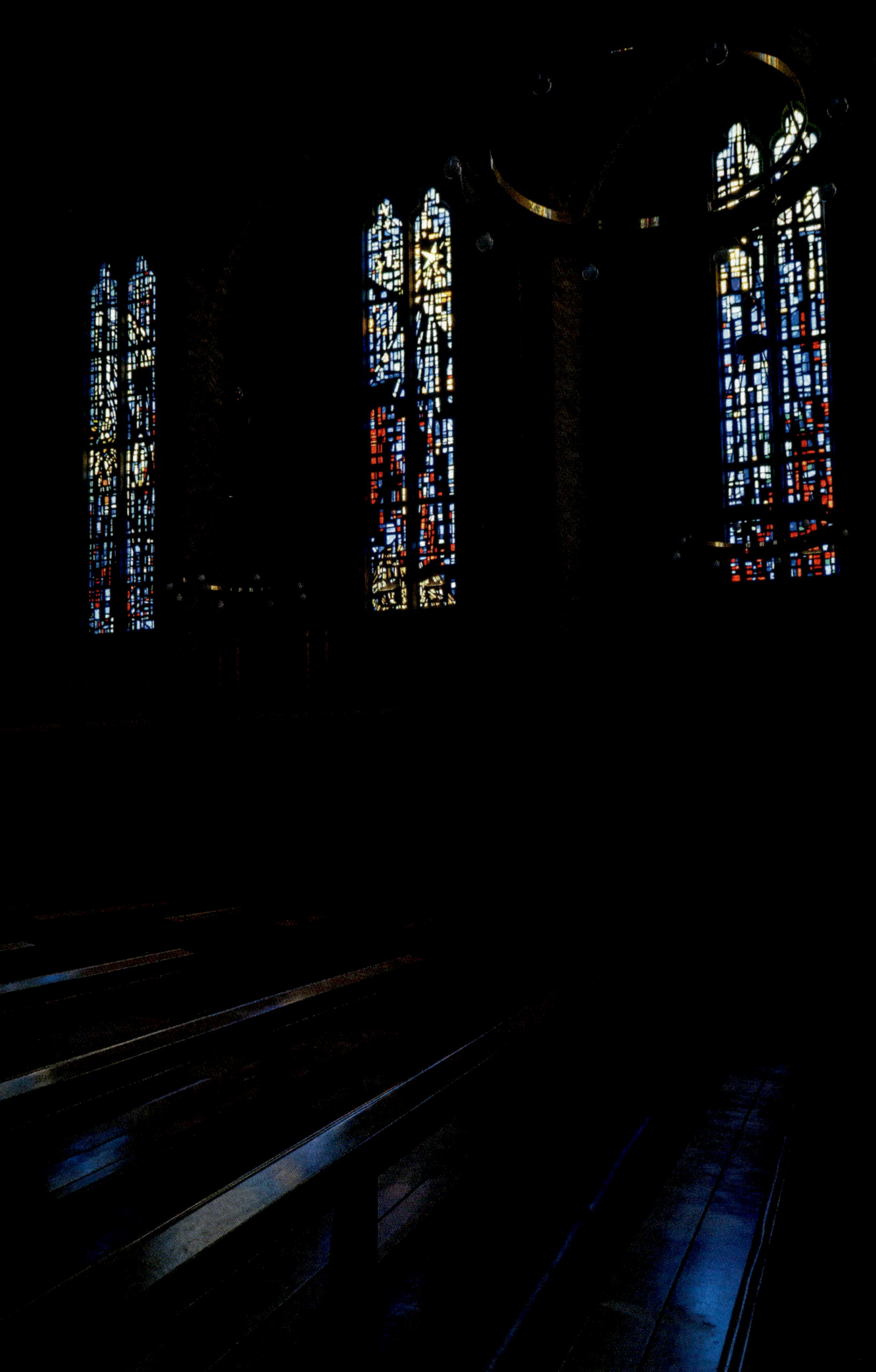

About the Author and Other Contributors

Bishop Richard Moth was ordained a priest for the Archdiocese of Southwark in 1982 and served as Bishop of the Armed Forces for six years before being appointed Bishop of Arundel I Brighton in 2015. He is Chair of the Board of Governors of St Mary's University. He has a long interest in Benedictine spirituality and is an Oblate of Pluscarden Abbey.

Sarah McKenna-Ayres is staff photographer at St Mary's University and founder of TigerBean Media, which focuses on portrait photography and creating artwork for the purposes of business promotion. Here she has a particular interest in architectural photography. She was one of the official photographers for the visit of HH Pope Benedict XVI to St Mary's in 2010.

Canon Dr Robin Gibbons is a fellow and the Alexander Schemann Professor of Eastern Christianity at the Graduate Theological Foundation in Mishawaka, Indiana; he was a faculty of theology member at the University of Oxford; and was formerly the Director of Studies for Theology and Religion in the department for continuing education at the University of Oxford. He was a senior lecturer in liturgy and historical theology at St Mary's for many years and is presently a Canon of the Anglican Cathedral of Oxford and a Melkite priest.

Professor Anthony McClaran has been Vice-Chancellor of St Mary's University since 2020, having previously been Chief Executive Officer of the Tertiary Education Quality and Standards Agency (TEQSA) of Australia, the Quality Assurance Agency for HE (QAA) and the Universities and Colleges Admissions Service (UCAS). He is currently a member of the board of AVEPRO, the Holy See's agency for the quality assurance of ecclesiastical HE institutions.

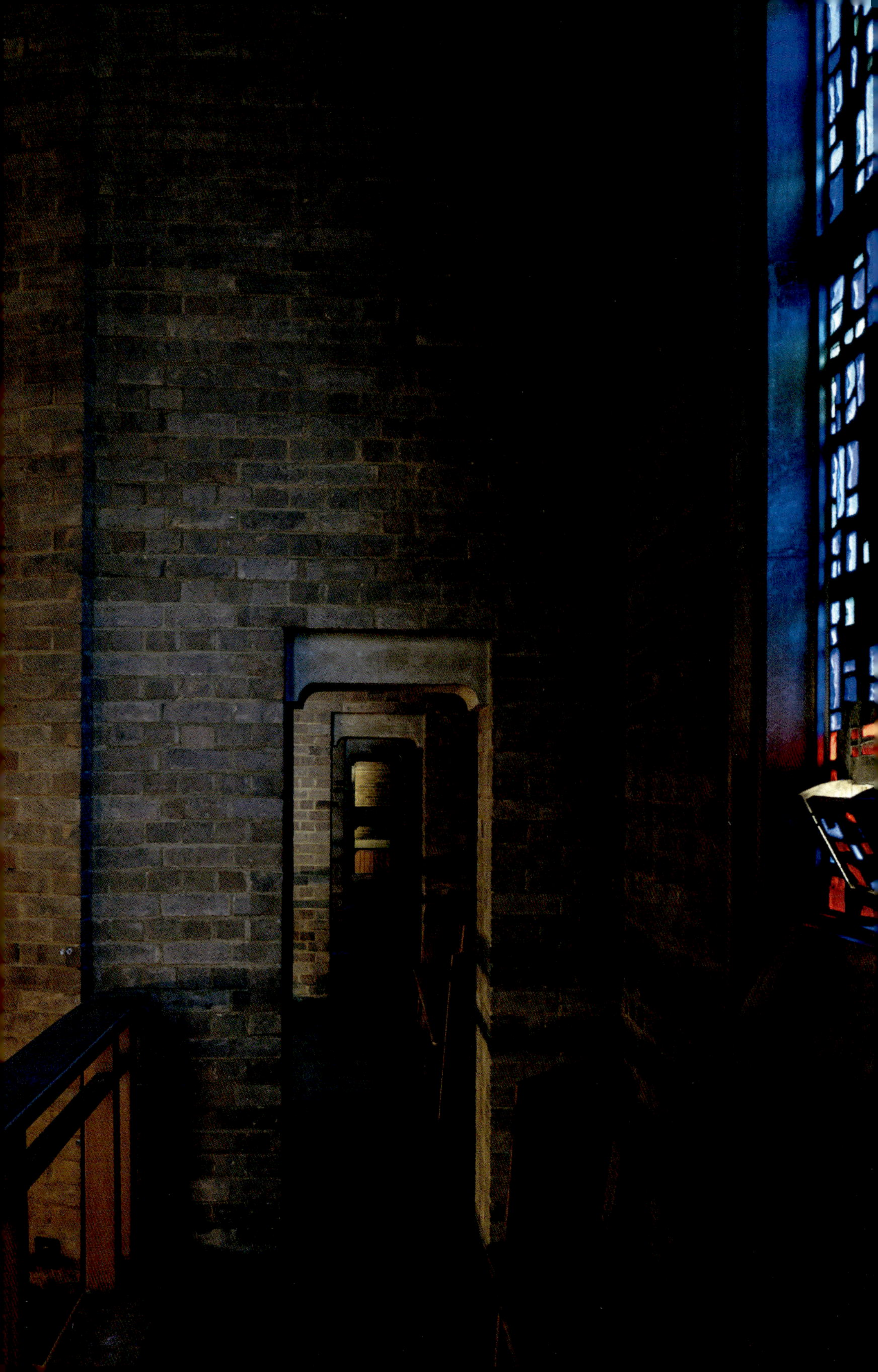

Monstra te esse Matrem

Show thyself to be our Mother

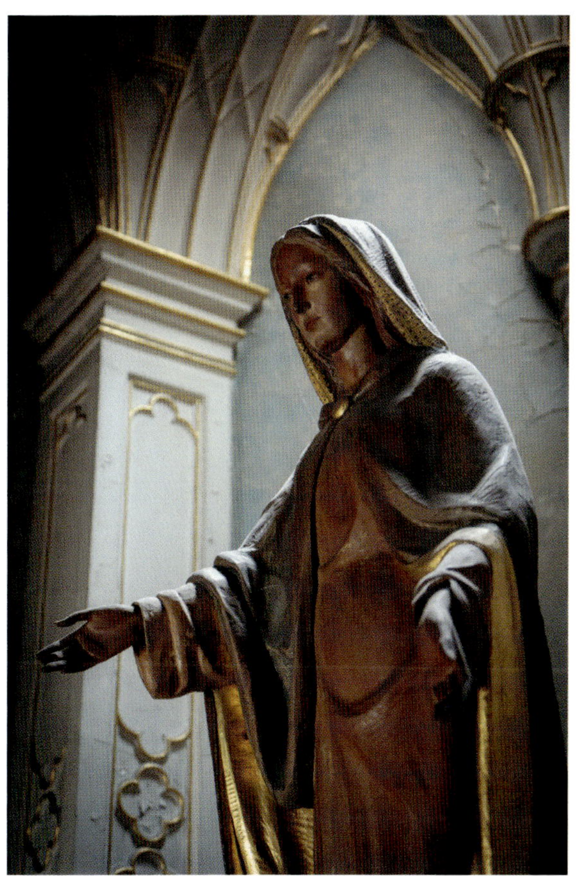

'Our Lady of Strawberry Hill',
Chapel in the Wood, St Mary's University